Earth Materials

Developed at

Lawrence Hall of Science

University of California at Berkeley

Published and Distributed by **Delta Education**

ISBN-10: 1-58356-836-0
ISBN-13: 978-1-58356-836-1

542-2002

Printing 9 – 5/2011
Quad/Graphics, Leominster, MA

TABLE OF CONTENTS

WRITTEN IN STONE

Dear Luis,

Remember how you worried about my vacation with Aunt Rita, the geologist? "She has to work," you said. "You'll be so bored." Were you ever wrong! Let me tell you what I've been doing.

Part of Aunt Rita's job reminds me of a scavenger hunt. She doesn't look for things on a list, though. Aunt Rita goes out into the country and makes a list of everything she sees. She collects facts for the U.S. Geological Survey. They publish maps and information that tell people where rocks, minerals, and resources are found.

Aunt Rita

Last week, we hunted for rock formations. Aunt Rita uses a field notebook to record how long, wide, and high each rock is. She looks to see whether it's angled or level. Then she plots its position on a map. I help her describe the different rocks. I look at their colors, textures, and shapes. I even have a hand lens to use while I'm here. That way, I can look at the rocks more closely. Sometimes it helps me if I can see the crystals on a rock's surface.

Aunt Rita studies rocks to learn their histories. When she picks up a rock, she tries to figure out what it's made of

A rock outcrop

and how and when it was formed. She wants to learn what has happened to the rock, too. Where did it come from? Has it moved around? Was it carried by a glacier or in a landslide? Did it travel in a stream? Think about it. A stone you pick up in your backyard has already had a whole lot of adventures!

Sedimentary rock

The other day, we were out in a flat, dry desert. The only thing growing was a kind of short, scrubby bush. But Aunt Rita looked at the rocks and said that the ground right where I was standing had once been underwater! Are you wondering how she knew? It was because we found sedimentary rocks there. "These rocks were made from tiny bits of shells and calcite," Aunt Rita told me. She said the shells and calcite had settled to the bottom of the sea that used to be there. Over time, they were pressed together and turned into rock.

I'm bringing a piece of a sedimentary rock back for you. That's another thing Aunt Rita does. She uses a rock hammer to break off samples of the rocks. She puts them in a sample bag and notes where they came from. Then she brings them back to a lab so she can study them up close.

My favorite afternoon so far is the one we spent by a river. The water had worn a channel into the rock, and we could see different layers. When we counted the layers, we were really counting how many times lava had flowed from a volcano. The rocks told Aunt Rita that at one time the volcano had exploded! Tiny particles had spewed out of the volcano in a huge, scorching cloud. The little particles were still so hot when they settled to the ground that they stuck together. Aunt Rita showed me the particles. I'd never imagined rock could form that way.

We also took a sample of lava rock from the riverbed to a lab. Aunt Rita said the sample was basalt. She wanted to look at it under a microscope. I watched her prepare the rock. First she sawed off a thin piece with a special saw. The piece was about a half-centimeter (quarter-inch) thick. She used a wheel covered with grit to smooth and polish one side of the piece. Then she glued the smooth side to a glass slide. She used the wheel again to grind down and polish the other side of the sample. Finally it was so thin that you could see light shine through it.

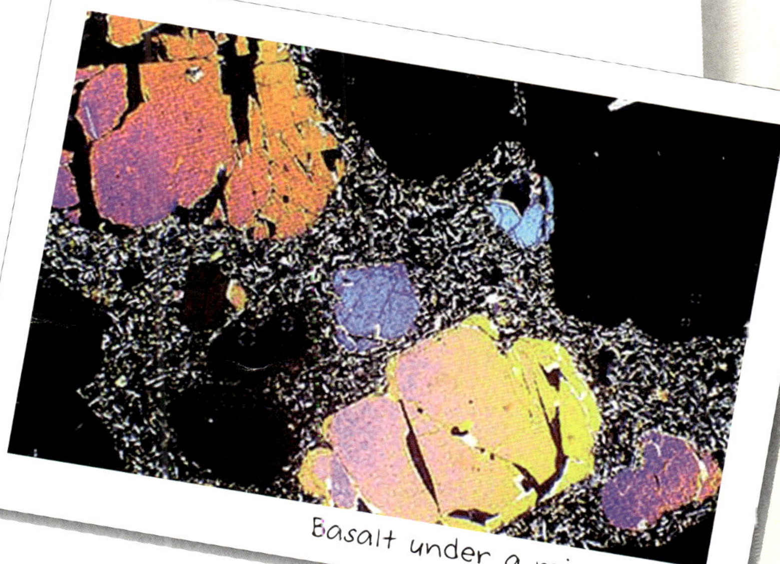

Basalt under a microscope

Aunt Rita put the slice of basalt under the microscope. I wish you could have seen it, Luis. It had a beautiful pattern of brightly colored shapes, like a stained glass window. Aunt Rita pointed out glassy particles and crystals to me. It's funny how something can look completely different when you look at it more closely.

While we were at the lab, I took out the piece of sedimentary rock I'm giving to you. If you look at it from the side, you can see layers. When I asked Aunt Rita about some dark spots, she got out a chisel and hammer. With a few careful taps, she split the rock where one layer laid over another. Guess what we found! The darker spots were fossils! Wait till you see them, Luis. There must be ten little fish. Each one is about 5 centimeters (2 inches) long. You can see a perfect outline of their bodies and bones. I can't imagine how long ago they died and fell to the bottom of that sea. Aunt Rita says the sea probably dried up before people even existed on the planet!

A fossil fish inside a rock

Another thing I'm doing here is making a rock collection. That will be my own little record of the Earth's past. Whenever I can, I'll write to you, too, Luis. That way, you'll have the history of my vacation.

Your friend,
Teresa

P.S. I thought you'd like to see these postcards Aunt Rita sent me over the last few years. There are a lot of interesting rocks in the world!

POSTCARDS FROM THE LEDGE

Devils Tower, Wyoming

Dear Teresa,

A story says seven Native American girls climbed onto a rock to escape a bear. As the bear jumped and scratched at its sides, the rock grew taller to keep the girls from harm. Doesn't Devils Tower look as if it formed that way? Northern Plains tribes call the tower "Bears Lodge." They consider it a sacred place. Devils Tower is really the core of a volcano. Rock around the core eroded away over millions of years.

In 1906, President Theodore Roosevelt named Devils Tower the first United States national monument!

Love, Aunt Rita

Moon Rocks
National Air and Space Museum
Washington, D.C.

Dear Teresa,

Did you know that astronauts collected more than 350 kilograms (800 pounds) of rock from the Moon? That means you don't have to travel through space to see Moon rocks up close. You can visit a museum here on Earth. Some Moon rocks are like Earth's basalt. Others are made of smaller rocks stuck together by heat.

Love, Aunt Rita

Sugar Loaf
Guanabara Bay, Brazil

Dear Teresa,

Sugar Loaf, or Pao de Açúcar, is part of an ancient mountain chain named the Serra do Mar. This granite mountain was named after a mold used to refine sugar. You wouldn't want to put granite on your cereal, though!

I think the mountain looks like half of a football. What do you think it looks like?

Love, Aunt Rita

Half Dome
Yosemite National Park, California

Dear Teresa,

Geologists say Half Dome is magma that cooled beneath the Earth's surface. Later it was uncovered by erosion.

At some point, huge sheets of granite fell off Half Dome. They were carried away by a glacier thousands of years ago. They may have been carried all the way down to the San Joaquin Valley, about 160 kilometers (100 miles) away! Pieces of rock just like Half Dome are found there.

Love, Aunt Rita

Teresa Campos
128 Big Rock Road
Orlando, FL 32856

Ship Rock
New Mexico

Dear Teresa,
You know that magma can reach the Earth's surface through a volcano. Can you guess what happens if the magma rises up into a volcano but doesn't flow out? It cools and turns into a hard mass of rock. Over time, the outer cone of the volcano may be worn away completely. Then all that's left is the magma that was inside the volcano. That's how Ship Rock was formed. From far away, pioneers crossing the country saw this inactive volcano as a ship sailing.
Love, Aunt Rita

Ayers Rock • 3.5 kilometers long, 345 meters high (2.2 miles long, 1,142 feet high)
Uluru-Kata Tjuta National Park, Australia

Dear Teresa,
A single large piece of rock is called a monolith. Ayers Rock is one of the largest monoliths in the world! It is made of sandstone. Because sandstone is not very hard, erosion makes interesting shapes and caves in the rock. The cave walls have paintings that were made thousands of years ago by Aborigines, native Australians. They call Ayers Rock "Uluru." To them, it is a sacred place. They tell stories about their ancestors and the rock.
Can you guess why Uluru is red? It rusted! That is, iron in the sandstone rusted. The rust gives the rock its color.
Love, Aunt Rita

QUESTIONS TO EXPLORE

- **Where would you go to look for rocks?**
- **If you could visit one of the rocks that Aunt Rita visited, which one would you choose, and why would you go there?**
- **Are there any "famous" rocks near you?**

TREASURE UNDERFOOT

Did you know there is treasure beneath you? Some of the most useful things on the Earth come from under its surface. Your jewelry, your bicycle, the walls and windows of your house, the cans that hold your food, and the dishes in your kitchen all come from the materials that make up the Earth.

People have taken minerals from the ground for thousands of years. They have turned them into tools, pottery, and jewelry. At first, people used shovels to move the layer of soil covering the minerals. They dug mines underground using picks. Sometimes the mines reached down hundreds of meters into hillsides and mountains. Miners carried minerals to the surface through narrow passages. It was a dirty and dangerous job. At times, children were forced to do the work.

Panning for gold

Gold mining machinery

Today mining is done in many ways. People mine underground and in open pits. They move earth with excavating machines and backhoes. Mechanical shovels with spinning teeth cut through rock. Explosive charges break rock into pieces. The way people mine depends on the mineral they are digging up. It also depends on where the mineral is found.

It's Not Too Late to Join the Gold Rush!

You can join the gold rush! Many federal and state lands are open to gold mining. Modern prospectors try their luck in states such as California, Washington, and Oregon. They pan for fun in historic mine area rivers and streams. Sometimes special events are held in places such as Tuckahoe State Park in Maryland and the Oakland Museum in California. Kids are taught how to pan for gold there.

Hard Facts DID YOU KNOW?

- The first iron used to make tools was not mined but came from meteorites.
- "Cleopatra's Mines" were rediscovered in 1818 in the desert south of Cairo. In ancient times, Egypt supplied the world with emeralds.
- A large amount of gold was found in North America between 1850 and 1875. It was more gold than was found in the world in the 350 years before that.
- Only about one in 1,000 prospectors ever struck gold in the western United States.
- Miners threw away tons of bluish rock as they dug for gold in the Utah Territory. In 1859, that rock was identified as silver ore!
- More than half the world's gold mined since 1886 has come from the coast of South Africa.

X Marks the Spot

In our time, science helps us detect useful resources. Geologists use special instruments on the ground and in airplanes. They even use artificial satellites to study the Earth.

In the past, however, valuable minerals were often found by accident or because they lay near the surface. Sometimes a single diamond or nugget of gold led the way to a major deposit.

Hope Town Gazette
Hope Town, South Africa
October 21, 1867

Farm Boys Discover a Valuable Diamond

Two local boys have found treasure. Erasmus Jacobs brought home a "pretty stone" last week. It proved to be a 21-carat diamond! The diamond had been lying in the dirt of a Hope Town farm near the bank of the Orange River. A boy from the Khoikhoi tribe picked it up and gave it to Erasmus. The diamond is about the size of a marble. It has been named Eureka.

Cape Town Times
Cape Town, South Africa
November 5, 1869

Another Hope Town Diamond Find

(Hope Town) It has been just two years since a boy found a diamond here. Now Booi, a young Griqua sheepherder, has found another. He thought it was a nice stone. He tried to use it to buy a night's lodging at an inn but was turned away. Later Booi traded the stone for ten oxen, 500 sheep, a horse, and a wagon. The stone turned out to be an 83.5-carat diamond! It has been named the Star of South Africa. People suspect there may be more diamonds in the area.

July 21, 1897

Gold in the Klondike!

San Francisco, California Two steamers from Alaska arrived here this week. They carried so much gold that one witness claimed it lay stacked in staterooms like suitcases. Lucky prospectors on board had learned of a gold strike made by George Washington Carmack. Carmack was born in California. He went north to Alaska to fish for salmon. Last August, he discovered gold in Rabbit Creek. Carmack's father was a forty-niner in the California gold rush. Now thousands are sure to travel north in a new stampede for gold.

Rabbit Creek has been renamed Bonanza Creek. It lies between the Klondike and Indian Rivers in Alaska.

NEW YORK GAZETTE

APRIL 3, 1849

Gold Discovered in California!

On January 24 of last year, James Marshall was building a water channel for a mill. He saw something yellow and shiny in the water. It was only about half the size of a pea. Marshall knew right away what it was.

"Boys..." he told his workers, "I believe I have found a gold mine."

Marshall's partner owns the land with the gold. His name is John Sutter. Sutter's Mill is on the American River in the Sacramento Valley of California.

People are rushing to this new part of the United States to find more gold.

Go to California and Strike It Rich

In the East, the rate of pay is one dollar for each day's work. In California, panning for gold may bring between 15 and 30 dollars a day. Some prospectors claim to find hundreds of dollars' worth of gold daily! They search for gold in streams and dried-up riverbeds. The gold is found as flakes, dust, and nuggets. It was washed there by erosion. One lucky searcher said, "All you need is a shovel, a washing pan, and the will to work."

Gold Fever

President James Polk spoke to the U.S. Congress last December. He told of large amounts of gold in California. Word quickly spread around the world. Thousands of people have been struck with "gold fever." They travel to California from the settled parts of the U.S. They journey from Central and South America. They come from all parts of Europe. They even come from places as far away as Asia and Australia. They all are seeking their fortunes in the riverbeds and gold mines of California.

DIGGING IT UP: MINING FOR MINERALS

GOLD

A gold-covered statue of Buddha

The methods used to retrieve gold from the ground and water have changed since the 1800s. Gold lies underground in veins running through other rock. A tunnel is dug to bring it to the surface. Special machines crush the rock. The gold is then processed and removed.

When gold erodes out of the mountains, it is carried away by water. It often comes to rest in stream beds. In earlier times, people mined gold by *panning* in streams. When sediment is swirled in a pan with water, the gold moves to the bottom of the pan. That's because it is heavier than other materials.

Modern ways of collecting gold sediment still depend on its heaviness. Sometimes a stream of water is used to sort the gold from the sediment as it washes over special channels. Flat-bottomed boats with buckets are also used to collect sediment. The sediment is poured into a screened container, which is spun. Water helps separate the gold from the other materials.

Gold is valued because it does not rust, wear away, or lose its bright color. It is soft, so it can be hammered or rolled into very thin sheets, stretched into wires, or shaped. To make coins or jewelry that will last, gold must be mixed with other harder metals. Gold is also used in dentistry and medicine.

GYPSUM

Gypsum is a soft mineral left behind when sea water evaporates. In some places, gypsum deposits are very thick. To reach a gypsum deposit, it may be necessary to remove a surface layer of mud or soil. Next gravel and rocks are removed. Then holes are drilled for explosives. Front end loaders take the chunks of blasted gypsum to be crushed.

When ground gypsum is heated, a fine powder called *plaster of Paris* is left behind. When mixed with water, plaster of Paris quickly swells and hardens. It is useful in making casts for things such as dental plates, ceramics, and statues. Gypsum is also used to make wallboard for building construction.

BAUXITE

Unloading bauxite ore

Bauxite is a rock made of soft minerals. It is found in clay. Bauxite deposits are found on or near the Earth's surface. In open-pit mines, mechanical shovels or rotary bucket excavators dig out bauxite. The bauxite is crushed, screened, and milled. Then heat, electricity, and a chemical process separate aluminum out of the bauxite.

Aluminum is a useful metal. It is three times lighter than steel and almost as strong. It is a good material for building bridges, aircraft, bicycles, and cars. Because it does not tarnish or rust, aluminum is made into siding for houses and hulls for boats. It is also formed into wire, insulation, cans, kitchenware, and foil for wrapping food.

IRON

Pure iron is soft. It becomes stronger when it is mixed with other materials. In ancient times, iron was used for ornaments, weapons, and tools. In the 1800s, it was used to make railroad rails, train car wheels, nails, and machine parts. Now most iron is used to make steel. Steel is good for building because it is very strong. It can be shaped into sheets, wires, beams, and pipes. Steel is used to make tools, blades, and cooking utensils.

The Empire State Building's steel skeleton

Iron ore is often collected from open-pit mines. The rock is broken by blasts of dynamite. Hydraulic power shovels lift the ore into huge trucks. The ore must be crushed and smelted to extract the iron. Today we use planes to find iron. The planes carry *magnetometers*, which sense changes in the Earth's magnetic field in places where there are large iron deposits.

BIRTHSTONES: A MINERAL FOR EACH MONTH

For a long time, people have identified stones with the months of the year. Such stones are called *birthstones* because each represents a month in which a person was born. Most birthstones are crystal versions of minerals. When cut and polished, they can be used as jewelry.

At one time, people believed birthstones could protect, heal, or bring good luck. Sometimes magical powers were associated with the stones. Though these ideas are not true, some people still believe them.

January: Garnet

Often colored red, garnet crystals form easily in rock. They need no polishing. Long ago, people believed a garnet would protect its owner from wounds.

February: Amethyst

Amethyst is a form of quartz that's purple. Amethysts were once thought to keep soldiers safe in battle.

March: Aquamarine

The mineral beryl forms crystals of different colors. Blue ones are called aquamarines. Aquamarines were supposed to bring good luck to sailors at sea.

April: Diamond

It takes extreme heat and pressure to turn carbon into diamond. Diamond is the hardest natural substance in the world. Some people believed a diamond would give them unbeatable strength.

May: Emerald

Unlike many other gemstones, emeralds are not found washed into streams. They must be mined from other rock. It was said that an emerald placed under the tongue let one see the future.

June: Alexandrite

Along with pearl, alexandrite is the birthstone for June. This mineral is both rare and unique. In natural sunlight, it looks green, but when lit by a light bulb, it appears to be red.

July: Ruby

Most rubies are found mixed with sediment in stream beds or under soil. It was thought that a ruby turning dark warned its owner of danger.

August: Peridot

Green and yellow-green peridots are forms of the mineral olivine. They can be found in lava flows and in meteorites. Peridot is the only gemstone from outer space! Peridot was said to give its wearer dignity.

September: Sapphire

Both sapphires and rubies are really crystals of the same mineral, corundum. The presence of different elements makes rubies red and sapphires blue. Legend claims a sapphire will make a foolish person wise.

October: Opal

Opals are a kind of mineral gel that contain water. Opals can be clear, cloudy, or *opaque*. Opals of good quality may show rainbowlike colors. The Romans wore opals for love and for hope.

November: Topaz

Pure topaz is colorless. The presence of certain elements can make topaz yellow, blue, green, orange, or pink. In the Middle Ages, topaz was said to improve the mind. The largest known topaz crystal weighs 271 kilograms (596 pounds)!

December: Turquoise

Blue-green turquoise is an opaque stone that is rarely found in crystal form. Native Americans of the Navajo tribe believed a turquoise thrown into a river with a prayer would bring rain.

Scratch Match

The diamond is the hardest birthstone. How do you think the other birthstones measure up? Here is a list of birthstones from hardest to least hard.

- Diamond
- Ruby and sapphire
- Topaz
- Alexandrite
- Aquamarine and emerald
- Amethyst and peridot
- Garnet
- Opal
- Turquoise

ROCK TALES

People have always been curious about the world around them. What raised the mountains? Why do rocks come in so many different colors, textures, and shapes? Why are some rocks found in one area but not in another? Once, questions like these seemed impossible to answer. No human watched the Earth being formed. How could things that happened so long ago be understood?

Today we know that the world is shaped by natural forces like volcanoes, earthquakes, and erosion. Long ago, people handed down stories from generation to generation to explain how the world and things in it came to be. These two legends about our Earth come from people on opposite sides of the world.

OLD MAN AND THE ROCK

A Native American Tale

Old Man was going along. As he went, he made the rivers and the mountains. He formed the animals and the people. He covered the plains with grass. And when he grew tired, Old Man stopped near a large rock.

Now the sun was beating down that day, and the rock was hot. Old Man threw his robe over the rock before he climbed up to nap. And after he woke, Old Man was so warm that he decided to leave his robe behind.

"You have let me rest on you," he said to the rock. All the things Old Man had made could understand him when he spoke. "Take my robe as a gift. Keep it always."

Then Old Man went on his way.

Soon it began to rain. Old Man did not like to get wet. When he met a coyote, he spoke to it.

"Little brother," he said. "See that large rock back there? Run to it. Ask it to lend me its robe."

The coyote did as he was told. But when he came back, he did not bring the robe.

"The rock says it needs the robe to keep out of the rain," the coyote said.

It made Old Man angry to think of the rock staying dry while he got wet. So he went back himself and pulled the robe off the rock.

"You will be out in the rain all your life," he said to the rock. "The rain will not hurt you. I only wished to borrow this robe that I gave you. But because you were too mean to share it, I will take it back."

Then Old Man went off with the coyote. With his robe, he made a tent to keep the two of them dry. Soon they were quite comfortable. But when the rain stopped, they heard a strange noise.

Old Man told the coyote, "Go up on the hill, brother, and see what makes such a sound."

The coyote went. Soon he came back, shouting as he ran. "Hurry away! The rock is coming!" Coyote had just enough time to crawl into a badger hole before the rock rolled over him. It was headed right for Old Man!

Old Man left the tent he had made and ran as fast as he could. "Help me!" he cried as he went.

All the creatures Old Man had made heard him. Nearest was a herd of buffalo. They ran and butted the rock with their heads. But the rock did not stop.

Then some deer and antelope tried to help. It did no good. The rock only went faster.

"Help me!" Old Man called again. "The rock is getting closer!"

Next rattlesnakes formed a lasso and threw themselves around the rock. Still the rock did not stop. Now it was hitting Old Man's heels as he ran.

"Help me!" Old Man cried once more. "Soon I will be crushed!"

The nighthawks saw that the rock could not be stopped, so they did not even try. Instead they flew at the rock with their sharp bills. *Chip, chip, chip!* They broke pieces off the rock until it began to grow smaller. At last, the rock was so tiny that when it rolled over Old Man, it did not hurt him.

Old Man was happy. Before he went on his way, he pinched the bills of the nighthawks to make them handsome. And that is why they look the way they do today, and also why the plains are covered with pebbles.

THE TWO BOYS

An Aborigine Story from Australia

Out in the sandy desert sits the great rock Uluru. If you went there, you might wonder why it towers into the sky. You might study its strange shapes and ask about the boulders on its slopes. Let me tell you how Uluru came to be.

One day in Dreamtime, the Two Boys went hunting. In that long ago time, the world was a flat place. There were no mountains, no trees, and no bushes. The Two Boys could see in every direction. When they spotted the Mala people, they were curious. They knew nothing of their ways and decided to see what the Mala were doing.

The Two Boys found the Mala gathered near a water hole. They watched the Mala men plant the ceremonial pole in the ground. From that moment on, everything the Mala did was part of the ceremony, or *inma*.

First the Mala separated into camps. One for the young men, one for the old. One for the single women, another for the married. Next the Mala went about their jobs. They collected water. They gathered and prepared food. All was done in its proper inma way.

The Two Boys soon grew tired of watching the Mala. They began to splash in the water hole. In no time at all, they turned the earth into mud. The mud was red. They piled it until it was very high. Then they climbed up on it to play. They slid down its sides and dragged their fingers along it. They called the mud mountain *Uluru*.

While the Two Boys did this, another people arrived from the west. They asked the Mala to join them in an inma. But the Mala would not. Their own inma had begun and could not be stopped. This made the people from the west angry. They went away and laid a branch and some sticks on the ground. They added the teeth of a mole and the tail of a bandicoot. When they were done, they sang songs over the creature they had made.

That night, while the Two Boys and the Mala slept, the creature came to life. It was the spirit dingo, Kurpany. In the morning, it went off to the Mala camps.

How frightened the Mala were! Kurpany chased them this way and that. To save themselves, the Mala changed everything, even themselves, into stone. To this day, you can see the Mala scattered over the slopes of Uluru. You can spot the food they cooked and the women's digging stick. You can see where the men took down the ceremonial pole and dragged it across the ground. You can even find parts of Kurpany and the footprints he made as he chased the Mala!

And what, you ask, became of the Two Boys? Why, after they escaped Kurpany, they turned north and went on with their hunt.

ROCK OF AGES

Humans want to remember the past. They also want to be remembered. Sometimes people build *memorials* or *monuments* so that other people will remember them. From ancient times to the present, people have made buildings with rock and stone because they last. Some rocks are nearly as old as the Earth itself. Some buildings made of stone have been standing for thousands of years.

Granite

If you stick to your ideas, someone might say you have a "will of granite." That compares you to a very hard rock. Granite is made from magma that cooled slowly deep beneath the Earth's surface.

Granite is the foundation rock of the continents. It is harder than the limestone of the Great Pyramid. It is also harder than marble, the building stone for the Taj Mahal and the Washington Monument. Granite holds up against weather. That makes it a good choice for building monuments and memorials.

The Sphinx and the Great Pyramid

TO PREPARE FOR AN AFTERLIFE: THE GREAT PYRAMID

Did you know that the Great Pyramid in Egypt is solid? The only hollow spaces are a few hallways and rooms. The pyramid was made with about 2,300,000 blocks of limestone and granite! The average block weighs about as much as two cars. The largest blocks are six times heavier.

Other Pyramids

Pyramids were not just built in Egypt. They were built in the Americas, too. They were often used as temples. Sometimes they were used as tombs, as well.

New World pyramids do not look exactly like most Egyptian pyramids. Many are flat-topped and stepped, such as the pyramid shown here, from Chichen Itza in Mexico.

In Egypt, a modern pyramid honors former leader Anwar al-Sadat (1918–1981). Its stone sides are covered with words from the *Koran,* Islam's holy book.

As big as it is, the Great Pyramid was made to honor just one person. It was built around 2700 B.C.E. to hold the body of the pharaoh Khufu. He was a ruler of ancient Egypt. The pyramid also held objects for him to use in the afterlife.

Each stone for the pyramid was pulled to the site on a wooden sled. Workers used copper axes, chisels, and saws to cut and fit the stones. Today people wonder how such a building could be made without iron tools or complex machines.

Limestone for the pyramid's core was cut out of nearby cliffs. That way, the stone did not have to be moved very far. Granite for the walls and doorways of the few rooms came from Aswan. That was almost 1,000 kilometers (600 miles) up the Nile River. Better limestone for the outside of the pyramid was ferried along the river from a few kilometers away. Today that original limestone shell is gone. The stone was "recycled" in the 1300s to rebuild a city damaged by earthquakes.

SHOWING ITS AGE: THE SPHINX

The Great Sphinx was carved 4,500 years ago from an outcropping of sandstone. It is being worn away by wind, humidity, and smog from the city of Cairo. It would be gone today if it hadn't spent most of its existence buried in the sand.

The Sphinx has the body of a lion and the head of a man. Some people believe the head looks like the pharaoh Khafre. He was buried in a nearby pyramid. The Sphinx is missing its nose. Its beard is in the British Museum. The Sphinx continues to slowly wear away. This is mainly from water damage from a nearby drainage system. A recent work project helped support the paws, legs, and abdomen of the Sphinx and make them stronger. The project took 10 years and over 12,000 limestone blocks.

TO MOURN A MUCH-LOVED WIFE: THE TAJ MAHAL

White marble was transported 500 kilometers (300 miles) to build the Taj Mahal in Agra, India. For 16 of those kilometers (10 miles), it was pulled by elephants and oxen along a specially made ramp.

The Taj Mahal

Both the Great Pyramid and the Taj Mahal are tombs. A pharaoh planned the Great Pyramid as his own burial place. The Taj Mahal's builder did not mean to use it himself. Emperor Shah Jahan wanted to remember one of his wives. She was Mumtaz Mahal, who died in 1630. Shah Jahan said his own tomb should be built nearby. It was to be connected to the Taj Mahal by a silver bridge. Shah Jahan's son seized power before this plan could be carried out. When Shah Jahan died, he was buried in the Taj Mahal beside Mumtaz Mahal.

Inside the Taj Mahal, colored marble was cut and pieced together like a puzzle. Forty-three different kinds of gemstones were used for decoration. The walls of the Taj Mahal are not solid like the Great Pyramid. They are layers of marble filled with rubble. The huge dome has a smaller dome inside it. The space between them is hollow.

To Remember the War Veterans:

The Vietnam Memorial

The Taj Mahal, the Great Pyramid, and the Washington Monument each honor a single person. The Vietnam Veterans Memorial was built to remember all the Americans who died in the Vietnam War (1955–1975). It was the idea of Vietnam veteran Jan Scruggs. A competition was held to design the memorial. Maya Ying Lin's plan was chosen. At the time, Lin was only 21 years old. She was a student at Yale University. She sent in a design as part of a class assignment. Lin designed the monument as a black granite wall. She wanted the stone to rise up like two hands to embrace people. The names of more than 58,000 military men and women are written on the wall. It was finished in 1982. The wall forms a V. One end points to the Washington Monument. The other end points to the Lincoln Memorial. Though many people criticized Lin's plan, the memorial she designed is one of the most visited sites in Washington, D.C., today.

The Vietnam Veterans Memorial in Washington, D.C., and its designer, then 21-year-old Maya Ying Lin.

How Do They Stack Up?

- People believe the Taj Mahal and the Great Pyramid each took about 20 years to build. Compare that to the Empire State Building. The skyscraper was completed in just 1 year and 45 days!
- Limestone was used for both the Great Pyramid and the Empire State Building. However, the Empire State Building is not solid limestone. It has a steel skeleton. Workers built that skeleton in a record 23 weeks!
- With 102 floors, the Empire State Building was the tallest building in the world for 39 years, from 1931 to 1970. The Great Pyramid held that honor for about 4,500 years! It's as tall as a modern 42-story building.

A TRIBUTE TO THE FIRST PRESIDENT:

THE WASHINGTON MONUMENT

The Washington Monument

George Washington died in 1799. That year, Congress voted to move his body to the capital city. They wanted to bury it under a marble monument. But Washington's body was never moved, and 85 years passed before a monument was completed. During that time, politicians fought. There were problems raising money for the monument. Sometimes there weren't enough railway cars to deliver marble. For 2 decades, work stopped altogether.

After the Civil War (1861–1865), there was interest in the monument again. People were worried about it. They said the base was not strong enough to support the finished building. Some of the marble blocks were splitting. The original plans had been lost. Many thought the monument was ugly. Some wanted to knock it down and start over. Others wanted a new design. Finally work went on after the foundation was made stronger. However, the new stone did not match the original. Visitors can see a color difference between the original marble from Maryland and the later marble from Maine. The great stone monument was finally completed in 1884.

One of the original plans for the Washington Monument

Did You Know?

- The observation room at the top of the Washington Monument can be reached by elevator or by climbing 898 steps.
- The Washington Monument is an *obelisk.* This form of building was often used in ancient Egypt. It is topped by a small pyramid.
- Only half of the planned monument for Washington was built. A Greek-style building was supposed to stand in front of the obelisk. Putting up the obelisk was such a problem that the second building was never constructed.

THE LONGEST CEMETERY IN THE WORLD: THE GREAT WALL

The 2,000-year-old Great Wall of China is an unofficial memorial to those who were forced to build it. It is the largest stone structure in the world. Legend says that for every stone used, a worker died. The bodies of many workers were buried beneath the heaviest stones.

The Great Wall was begun about 221 B.C.E. and it was finished about 204 B.C.E. The wall was constructed for defense. It runs for more than 2,400 kilometers (1,500 miles). If its loops and curves were stretched out, it would reach from Los Angeles to Chicago and back again. That's a distance of 5,600 kilometers (3,500 miles)! The Great Wall is so big that it's the only human-built structure that can be seen from a space shuttle in space.

The Great Wall of China

QUESTIONS TO EXPLORE

- **Suppose you could honor someone or something very special with a monument. Whom or what would you choose to honor? Where would you build the monument? What rock or mineral would you use to build it and why?**
- **What monuments are in your area? Whom or what do they honor? What are they made of and how were they made?**

IDENTIFYING MINERALS

Rocks are made out of earth materials called minerals. Minerals can be colorful and beautiful.

Minerals come in many colors. Starting with the brown mineral at the top and moving clockwise, the minerals shown here are copper, orpiment/realgar, beryl, malachite, sapphire, olivine, and cinnabar. The yellow mineral in the center is sulfur.

Many different kinds of rock can be made out of just a few kinds of minerals. Geologists try to find out what kinds of minerals are in rocks. They use property tables to help them identify the minerals they find in rocks. Here are some of the mineral properties they use.

Hardness: Hardness is determined by trying to scratch a mineral with different materials. Minerals with large hardness numbers, like 8, 9, or 10, can't be scratched. Even a steel knife won't scratch a hard mineral. Minerals with small hardness numbers, like 1, 2, and 3, are easy to scratch. Even a fingernail can scratch one of these minerals.

A scientist might use a nail to test the hardness of a mineral like this feldspar.

Specific Gravity: Specific gravity (SG) compares the mass of a mineral sample to the mass of an equal amount of water. Here's an example. A 5-cubic-centimeter sample of a mineral is twice as heavy as a 5-cubic-centimeter sample of water. In this example, the specific gravity is 2.

Color: Some minerals, like black biotite mica, have colors that help identify them. But some minerals come in many different colors. The property of color can't always be used to identify a mineral.

Fluorite is a mineral that comes in many different colors.

Light Properties: Minerals can be *transparent* (Tp), *translucent* (Tl), or *opaque* (Op). Transparent means you can see through a mineral. Translucent means some light can pass through a mineral. Opaque means no light at all can pass through.

In this picture, calcite is transparent. Fluorite is translucent. Iron pyrite is opaque.

Magnetism: A mineral is magnetic if small bits of iron stick to it.

Steel nails stick to this magnetic mineral.

Cleavage: Geologists look at how a mineral breaks when hit with a hammer. Regular, flat surfaces on broken minerals are called *cleavage*.

Cleavage surfaces are smooth and flat in this mineral.

Fracture: Uneven, rounded, or splintered surfaces on broken rocks are called *fractures*.

Rounded fractures on obsidian

Uneven fractures on quartz

Streak: If you rub a mineral on an unglazed white tile, it can leave a streak. The color of the streak can help a geologist identify the mineral.

The mineral hematite leaves a brown streak.

Common Rock-forming Minerals

Here are the properties of some common rock-forming minerals.

Mineral	Hardness	SG	Color	Light	Cleavage	Fracture	Streak
Gypsum	2	2.32	variable	Tp/Tl/Op	yes	splinters	white
Mica	3	3.10	black	Tp/Tl/Op	yes	uneven	colorless
Calcite	3	2.71	variable	Tp/Tl	yes	uneven	white
Fluorite	4	3.20	variable	Tp/Tl	yes	rounded	white
Hornblende	5	3.35	black	Op	yes	uneven	gray
Feldspar	6	2.60	variable	Tl	yes	uneven	white
Quartz	7	2.65	variable	Tp/Tl/Op	no	uneven	colorless

Ore Minerals

Ore minerals are mined for the metals they contain. Iron comes from hematite. Lead comes from galena.

Mineral	Hardness	SG	Color	Light	Cleavage	Fracture	Streak
Galena	2–3	7.58	dark gray	Op	yes	rounded	gray
Hematite	5	5.26	variable	Op	no	uneven	red/brown

Key: Tp = Transparent Tl = Translucent Op = Opaque SG = Specific gravity

WHERE DO ROCKS COME FROM?

Where do rocks come from? This question keeps geologists busy. Even though they don't have all the answers, they know a lot about where rocks come from.

There are three big groups of rocks. All the rocks in a group have similar origins. The three groups are *igneous, sedimentary,* and *metamorphic.*

Igneous rocks start out as melted rock deep under the surface of the Earth. Sometimes the melted rock comes to the surface in volcanoes. It pours out as lava. When the lava cools and hardens, it forms new rocks.

Other times the melted rock slowly cools and hardens below the surface. Earthquakes and other changes in the Earth's surface might bring these igneous rocks to the surface years later.

Igneous rocks can be crystalline or glassy. Granite is an example of an igneous rock. If you look at a granite sample with a hand lens, you can see the crystals of quartz, feldspar, and mica.

Obsidian is also an igneous rock. Obsidian is smooth and shiny, but has no crystals.

Sedimentary rocks start out as bits of recycled rocks and minerals. Sandstone is an example of a sedimentary rock. The story of sandstone starts with big rocks in mountains. Over time, the rocks crack and break down into smaller pieces. This process is called *weathering*. Water can cause weathering in rocks. Water freezes in cracks in rocks. When this happens, the cracks get bigger. When the water thaws, the rocks crumble. Tree roots also cause weathering in rocks. Roots may grow in cracks. As the roots grow, the cracks get bigger. As a result of these natural processes, big pieces of rock break loose. The rocks tumble downhill and break into smaller pieces. Smaller pieces end up in streams and rivers. The pieces are banged around and broken into smaller and smaller pieces. Eventually the rocks from the mountain are reduced to sand.

Sand often ends up in lakes and bays. It forms a layer on the bottom of the lake or bay. These layers of sand and other materials are called sediment. As millions of years pass, the sand gets buried under more layers of sediment. The sand particles are pressed and cemented together. The sand turns into sandstone. Other sedimentary rocks, like limestone and shale, form in similar ways.

Sedimentary rocks often have bits of sand and gravel you can see. Sometimes sedimentary rocks contain fossils of shells or plants. Sedimentary rocks form in layers. If the rocks are still in their natural site, you can see the layers.

Metamorphic rocks start out as masses of other rocks. They can be igneous, sedimentary, or even other metamorphic rocks. These rocks can change because of heat and pressure. Heat and pressure can come from different sources. The source might be a volcano or an earthquake. The heat and pressure change the rocks into another kind of rock.

Heat and pressure can turn sandstone into quartzite. They can turn limestone into marble. They can turn shale into slate. Look closely at a metamorphic rock. Sometimes you can see the crystals that formed when the metamorphic rock cooled.

The chart on the next page shows how to sort the five rocks you used in your investigations. It includes pictures of three more igneous, sedimentary, and metamorphic rocks.

Igneous

Granite

Basalt

Tuff

Pumice

Obsidian

Sedimentary

Limestone

Sandstone

Shale

Conglomerate

Breccia

Metamorphic

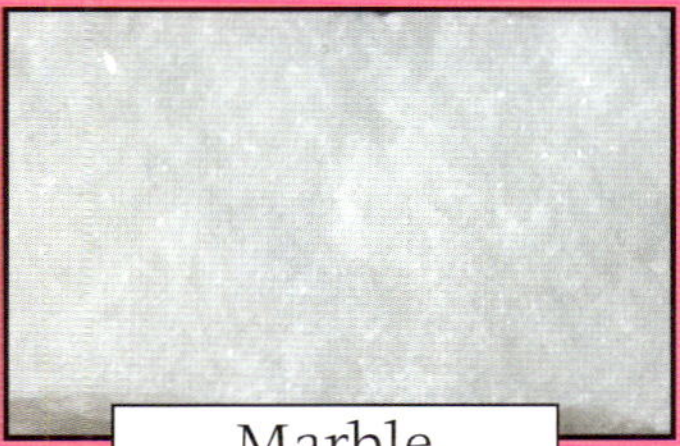
Marble

Slate

Gneiss

Schist

GLOSSARY

Carat A unit of weight for precious stones, equal to 200 milligrams (140 carats is equal to just under 1 ounce).

Crystal The solid form of a material that can be identified by its natural shape or pattern.

Deposit Earth material that has been laid down by the action of wind, water, ice, or volcanic eruption.

Erosion The wearing away of earth materials by water, wind, or ice.

Evaporate To dry up.

Excavate To dig out; to uncover by digging.

Fossil Any remains, trace, or imprint of prehistoric animal or plant life preserved in the Earth's crust.

Gemstone A mineral or other earth material that can be cut and polished to set in a piece of jewelry.

Geologist A person who studies the Earth and the materials of which it is made.

Glacier A large, slow-moving mass of ice and snow that forms in places where the rate of snowfall is faster than the rate the snow melts.

Igneous rock A rock that forms from molten or melted rock.

Magma Liquid or molten rock deep in the Earth; the lava ejected when a volcano erupts.

Magnetometer An instrument for measuring the Earth's magnetic field and its changes.

Memorial Anything meant to help people remember some person or event.

Metamorphic rock A rock that forms into another kind of rock by heat, pressure, or both.

Meteorite Any solid object that falls from outer space through a planet's atmosphere and lands on the surface.

Microscope An instrument with lenses that makes small objects appear larger so they can be studied.

Mineral A basic earth material; a rock ingredient that cannot physically be broken down any further.

Monolith A single large piece of stone.

Monument A structure built to help people remember some person or event.

Obelisk A tall, slender, four-sided stone pillar that has a pyramid on top.

Opaque Any substance or object that does not let light shine through; not transparent.

Outcrop A mass of rock exposed at the Earth's surface.

Prospector A person who searches for valuable resources such as ores, minerals, and oil.

Pyramid Any huge structure built with a square base and four sloping, triangular sides that meet at the top; also anything that has a similar shape.

Sediment Solid matter such as sand or gravel deposited by wind, water, and ice.

Sedimentary rock A layered rock formed by deposits of sediment.

Smelt To melt or fuse ores in order to separate pure metals from impurities.

Texture The surface properties of any material, especially as they apply to appearance or touch.

Vein A continuous crack in rock filled with one or more minerals, especially metallic ores, differing from the surrounding rock.